Cameron Mackintosh
presents

PIANO • VOCAL SELECTIONS

Les Misérables

© CMI 1986

THE MUSICAL SENSATION

1987 TONY® AWARD
BEST MUSICAL

Arranged by TODD LOWRY

W9-BUG-380

DATE DUE

By Alain Boublil and Claude-Michel Schönberg
Based on the novel by Victor Hugo

Music by Claude-Michel Schönberg – Lyrics by Herbert Kretzmer
Original French text by Alain Boublil and Jean-Marc Natel
Additional material by James Fenton

Associate Director and Executive Producer Richard Jay-Alexander
Executive Producer Martin McCallum
Casting by Johnson-Liff Associates – General Management Alan Wasser

Orchestral score by John Cameron
Musical supervision and direction by Robert Billig
Sound by Andrew Bruce/Autograph

Designed by John Napier – Lighting by David Hersey – Costumes by Andreane Neofitou

Directed and Adapted by Trevor Nunn & John Caird

HAL LEONARD
PUBLISHING
CORPORATION
Home Office: National Sales Office:
950 East Mark Street   8112 West Bluemound Road
Winona, MN 55987   Milwaukee, WI 53213

Alain Boublil
Photo: Michael Le Poer Trench

Claude-Michel Schönberg
Photo: Michael Le Poer Trench

Herbert Kretzmer

The idea of turning *LES MISÉRABLES* into a musical came to me one evening in 1979 during a visit to London, where I had come – naturally – to see musicals.

To the French, Victor Hugo's classic novel has the status of a national monument, and I was well aware at the outset that such an enterprise would be regarded by the guardians of our heritage as an act of desecration.

Nonetheless, I discussed the idea with my colleague, Claude-Michel Schönberg, with whom I had already tackled "The French Revolution". It seemed to both of us that here was a most exciting challenge, and a unique opportunity to work outside of the established conventions of musical theatre.

Hugo's original text lent itself very well to operatic treatment and, after nine months of hard work, we had transformed the 1500-page book into an opera libretto of three acts, seven tableaux – together with a detailed description of the music and lyrics of the whole score as we then imagined it. After much revision, we reached the point at which Claude-Michel could go away and start composing and I could begin work on the words. This I did – after myself deciding on the subject and title of every song – in collaboration with my friend Jean-Marc Natel, a poet and an expert on Hugo.

LES MISÉRABLES opened at the Palais des Sports in Paris in September of 1980, directed by Robert Hossein, for a 3 month season and would have been extended further had it not been for other bookings. The first production was seen by over a million people.

In 1982, Cameron Mackintosh heard the French album of LES MISÉRABLES, and invited Claude-Michel and myself, directors Trevor Nunn and John Caird, and James Fenton to rework an English version of our musical. Herbert Kretzmer joined us to create English counterparts of the original French lyrics, adding in the process some new lyrics specially for the English production.

LES MISÉRABLES was back again at the Barbican Theatre, London, on October 8th, 1985. It was an instant success and transferred on December 4th of that year to the Palace Theatre where it has been sold out ever since.

The Broadway production opened to enormous success on March 12th, 1987 and, like Hugo's original book, seems destined to reach a worldwide public.

This book of musical selections contains fourteen of our favorite songs from the production. I hope that the music and lyrics somehow convey the turmoil of France in the 1820s and 30s, and especially the epic, romantic quality of those times – so vividly captured by the genius of Victor Hugo – that inspired us in our musical recreation of a literary masterpiece.

ALAIN BOUBLIL
Paris, March 1987

Prologue: 1815, Digne

Jean Valjean, released on parole after 19 years on the chain gang, finds that the yellow ticket-of-leave he must, by law, display condemns him to be an outcast. Only the saintly Bishop of Digne treats him kindly and Valjean, embittered by years of hardship, repays him by stealing some silver. Valjean is caught and brought back by police, and is astonished when the Bishop lies to the police to save him, also giving him two precious candlesticks. Valjean decides to start his life anew.

1823, Montreuil-sur-Mer

Eight years have passed and Valjean, having broken his parole and changed his name to Monsieur Madeleine, has risen to become both a factory owner and Mayor. ('At The End Of The Day'). One of his workers, Fantine, has a secret illegitimate child. When the other women discover this, they demand her dismissal. The foreman, whose advances she has rejected, throws her out. ('I Dreamed A Dream')

Desperate for money to pay for medicines for her daughter, Fantine sells her locket, her hair, and then joins the whores in selling herself. Utterly degraded by her new trade, she gets into a fight with a prospective customer and is about to be taken to prison by Javert when 'The Mayor' arrives and demands she be taken to hospital instead.

The Mayor then rescues a man pinned down by a runaway cart. Javert is reminded of the abnormal strength of convict 24601 Jean Valjean, a parole-breaker whom he has been tracking for years but who, he says, has just been recaptured. Valjean, unable to see an innocent man go to prison in his place confesses to the court that he is prisoner 24601. (Who Am I?)

At the hospital, Valjean promises the dying Fantine to find and look after her daughter Cosette. Javert arrives to arrest him, but Valjean escapes.

1823, Montfermeil

Cosette has been lodged for five years ('Castle On A Cloud') with the Thénadiers who run an inn, horribly abusing the little girl whom they use as a skivvy while indulging their own daughter, Eponine. ('Master Of The House') Valjean finds Cosette fetching water in the dark. He pays the Thénadiers to let him take Cosette away and takes her to Paris. But Javert is still on his tail . . .

1832, Paris

Nine years later, there is great unrest in the city because of the likely demise of the popular leader General Lamarque, the only man left in the Government who shows any feeling for the poor. The urchin Gavroche is in his element mixing with the whores and beggers of the capital.

Among the street-gangs is one led by Thénadiers and his wife, which sets upon Jean Valjean and Cosette. They are rescued by Javert, who does not recognise Valjean until after he has made good his escape ('Stars'). The Théanadiers' daughter Eponine, who is secretly in love with student Marius, reluctantly agrees to help find Cosette, with whom he has fallen in love.

At a political meeting in a small café, a group of idealistic students prepare for the revolution they are sure will erupt on the death of General Lamarque. When Gavroche brings the news of the General's death, the students, led by Enjolras, stream out into the streets to whip up popular support. ('Do You Hear The People Sing?') Only Marius is distracted, by thoughts of the mysterious Cosette.

Cosette is consumed by thoughts of Marius, with whom she has fallen in love ('In My Life'). Valjean realizes that his 'daughter' is changing very quickly but refuses to tell her anything of her past. In spite of her own feelings for Marius, Eponine sadly brings him to Cosette ('A Heart Full Of Love') and then prevents an attempt by her father's gang to rob Valjean's house. Valjean, convinced it was Javert who was lurking outside his house, tells Cosette they must prepare to flee the country. On the eve of the revolution, the students and Javert see the situation from their different viewpoints; Cosette and Marius part in despair of ever meeting again; Eponine mourns the loss of Marius; and Valjean looks forward to the security of exile. The Thénadiers, meanwhile, dream of rich pickings underground from the chaos to come.

The students prepare to build the barricade. Marius, noticing that Eponine has joined the insurrection, sends her with a letter to Cosette, which is intercepted at the Rue Plumet by Valjean. Eponine decides, despite what he has said to her, to rejoin Marius at the Barricade. ('On My Own')

The barricade is built and the revolutionaires defy an army warning that they must give up or die. Gavroche exposes Javert as a police spy. In trying to return to the barricade, Eponine is shot and killed ('A Little Fall Of Rain') Valjean arrives at the barricades in search of Marius. He is given the chance to kill Javert but instead lets him go.

The students settle down for a night on the barricade ('Drink With Me') and in the quiet of the night, Valjean prays to God to save Marius from the onslaught which is to come. ('Bring Him Home') The next day, with ammunition running low, Gavroche runs out to collect more and is shot. The rebels are all killed, including their leader Enjolras.

Valjean escapes into the sewers with the unconscious Marius. After meeting Thénadier, who is robbing the corpses of the rebels, he emerges into the light only to meet Javert once more. He pleads for time to deliver the young man to hospital. Javert decides to let him go and, his unbending principles of justice having been shattered by Valjean's own mercy, he kills himself by throwing himself into the swollen River Seine.

A few months later, Marius, unaware of the identity of his rescuer, has recovered and recalls, at Cosette's side, the days of the barricade where all his friends have lost their lives. ('Empty Chairs At Empty Tables') Valjean confesses the truth of his past to Marius and insists that after the young couple are married, he must go away rather than taint the sanctity and safety of their union. At Marius and Cosette's wedding, the Thénadiers try to blackmail Marius. Thénadier says Cosette's 'father' is a murderer and as proof produces a ring which he stole from the corpse in the sewers the night the barricades fell. It is Marius' own ring and he realises it was Valjean who rescued him that night. He and Cosette go to Valjean where Cosette learns for the first time of her own history before the old man dies, joining the spirits of Fantine, Eponine and all those who died on the barricades.

"At The End Of The Day" – *The Company*

Randy Graff as Fantine
"I Dreamed A Dream"

"Castle On A Cloud"
Donna Vivino as Young Cosette

*Michael Maguire as Enjolras
at the Barricades*

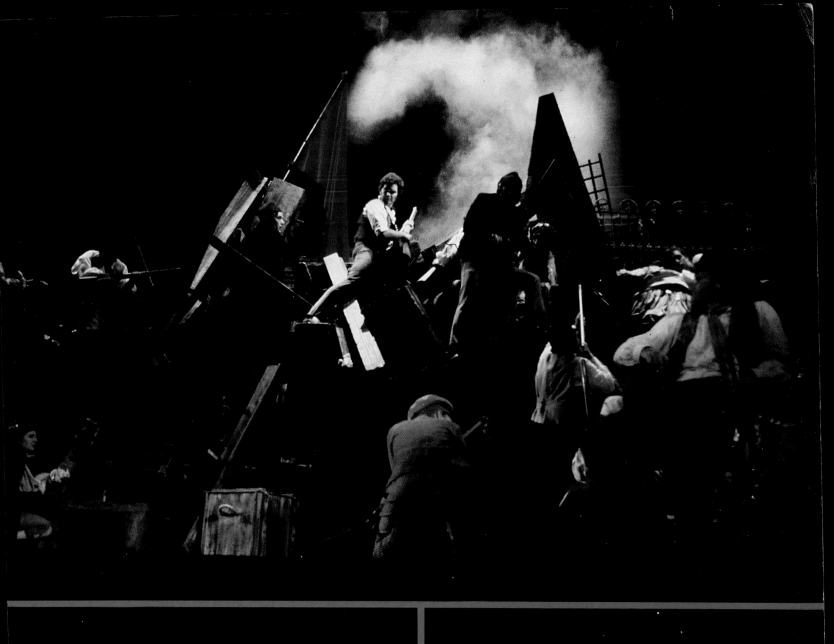

At The Barricades

Frances Ruffelle as Eponine

"A Little Fall Of Rain"
Marius (David Bryant),
Eponine (Frances Ruffelle)

"Drink With Me"
Grantaire (Anthony Crivello)
and Company

At The Barricade
"Bring Him Home"
*Colm Wilkinson as
Jean Valjean*

The Sewers Of Paris

Out Of The Sewers
Valjean (Colm Wilkinson)
carrying Marius (David Bryant)

Valjean (Colm Wilkinson) and Javert (Terrence Mann)

Master Of The House
Thenardier (Leo Burmester) and Company

"Finale" Act II – *The Company*

AT THE END OF THE DAY

Lyrics by HERBERT KRETZMER
Original text by ALAIN BOUBLIL and JEAN-MARC NATEL
Music by CLAUDE-MICHEL SCHÖNBERG

THE POOR:

At the end of the day you're an-oth-er day old-er.
At the end of the day you're an-oth-er day cold-er.

And that's all you can say for the life of the poor.
And the shirt on your back does-n't keep out the chill.

It's a
And the

I DREAMED A DREAM

Lyrics by HERBERT KRETZMER
Original text by ALAIN BOUBLIL and JEAN-MARC NATEL
Music by CLAUDE-MICHEL SCHÖNBERG

FANTINE:

I dreamed a dream in days gone by when hope was high and life worth

liv - ing. I dreamed that love would nev - er die.

I dreamed that God would be for - giv - ing. Then I was young and un - a -

WHO AM I?

Lyrics by HERBERT KRETZMER
Original text by ALAIN BOUBLIL and JEAN-MARC NATEL
Music by CLAUDE-MICHEL SCHÖNBERG

CASTLE ON A CLOUD

Lyrics by HERBERT KRETZMER
Original text by ALAIN BOUBLIL and JEAN-MARC NATEL
Music by CLAUDE-MICHEL SCHÖNBERG

Aren't an - y floors for me to sweep,
No - bod - y shouts or me talks to too loud,

not in my cas - tle on a cloud.
not in my cas - tle on a cloud.

There is a la - dy all in white, ___

holds me and sings a lul - la - by. She's nice to see and she's soft to touch. She

MASTER OF THE HOUSE

Lyrics by HERBERT KRETZMER
Original text by ALAIN BOUBLIL and JEAN-MARC NATEL
Music by CLAUDE-MICHEL SCHÖNBERG

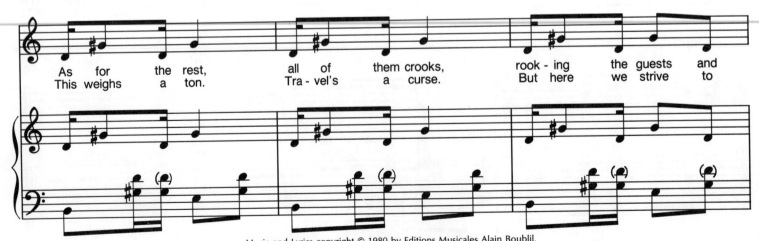

STARS

Lyrics by HERBERT KRETZMER and ALAIN BOUBLIL
Music by CLAUDE-MICHEL SCHÖNBERG

fall _____ in flame! And so it has

been and so it is writ-ten on the door - ways to Par-a-dise, ___ that those who

fal - ter and those who fall _____ must pay _____ the

price. _____

DO YOU HEAR THE PEOPLE SING?

Lyrics by HERBERT KRETZMER
Original text by ALAIN BOUBLIL and JEAN-MARC NATEL
Music by CLAUDE-MICHEL SCHÖNBERG

IN MY LIFE

Lyrics by HERBERT KRETZMER
Original text by ALAIN BOUBLIL and JEAN-MARC NATEL
Music by CLAUDE-MICHEL SCHÖNBERG

learn. Truth is giv-en by God to us all in our time, in our

turn.

MARIUS:

In my

life she has burst like the mu-sic of an-gels, the light of the sun. And my life seems to stop as if some-thing is o-ver and some-thing has scarce-ly be -

gun. E-po - nine, you're the friend that has brought me here. Thanks to

you I am one with the gods and hea-ven is near.

And I soar through a world that is new that is free.

piu mosso

A HEART FULL OF LOVE

Lyrics by HERBERT KRETZMER
Original text by ALAIN BOUBLIL and JEAN-MARC NATEL
Music by CLAUDE-MICHEL SCHÖNBERG

A LITTLE FALL OF RAIN

Lyrics by HERBERT KRETZMER
Original text by ALAIN BOUBLIL and JEAN-MARC NATEL
Music by CLAUDE-MICHEL SCHÖNBERG

DRINK WITH ME
(TO DAYS GONE BY)

Lyrics by HERBERT KRETZMER and ALAIN BOUBLIL
Music by CLAUDE-MICHEL SCHÖNBERG

BRING HIM HOME

Lyrics by HERBERT KRETZMER
and ALAIN BOUBLIL
Music by CLAUDE-MICHEL SCHÖNBERG

EMPTY CHAIRS AT EMPTY TABLES

Lyrics by HERBERT KRETZMER and ALAIN BOUBLIL
Music by CLAUDE-MICHEL SCHÖNBERG

ON MY OWN

Lyrics by ALAIN BOUBLIL, HERBERT KRETZMER,
JOHN CAIRD, TREVOR NUNN and JEAN-MARC NATEL
Music by CLAUDE-MICHEL SCHÖNBERG

80